MW00886779

The SELF Project for Parents

Kari O'Driscoll

Copyright © 2012 Kari O'Driscoll

All rights reserved.

ISBN: 1523920092
ISBN-13: 978-1523920099

DEDICATION

To all the people in my life who have acted as parents to me, and to those who still do, thank you for offering me love and patience and teaching me what it is to be cared for unconditionally. Mom? I'm so sorry for the teenage years. And to my daughters and their friends, thank you for allowing me to be part of your lives and learn from you as well. My life is so rich thanks to all of you amazing young people.

CONTENTS

Acknowledgments   i

1   Introduction   1

2   Important Information about the Adolescent Brain   Pg 3

3   Mindful Parenting   Pg 6

4   Trusting Relationships   Pg 11

5   Compassion   Pg 14

6   Shared Goals   Pg 19

7   Conflict   Pg 23

8   Helping Your Child Deal with Stress & Anxiety   Pg 27

ACKNOWLEDGMENTS

This book was made possible by a group of amazing writers whose work I follow and whose insights I have been blown away by. The friends and family who have supported me through this research and been my guinea pigs as I tested out new ideas on them are invaluable and I hope to one day be able to express my gratitude in a way that is meaningful.

1 INTRODUCTION

Any Social-Emotional Health curriculum that doesn't include parents or family caregivers is incomplete. Pretending that our children only learn during the hours when they are at school is, at best, short-sighted, and at worst, dangerous. And even if we can acknowledge that they are learning when they aren't in class, imposing an artificial separation between the kinds of things they learn at school and those they learn out in the world and at home doesn't serve any of us. It is important to recognize that our kids are part of a larger community that includes parents and extended family, classmates, teachers, coaches, employers and healthcare professionals. If we can all work together to teach our kids important things about how to stay emotionally healthy and find fulfillment in their lives, our communities will be stronger for it. This book can help with that because it was created alongside the curriculum for kids and teachers and can help family members reinforce those ideas when your child isn't in school.

These discussions and activities were designed to help you parent your adolescent through some of the most challenging years you will face together. Based on the most current research into the adolescent brain and rooted in practical, tested ideas about how to connect and nurture your child, it offers new ways to think about how we help shape our children as they grow up. Whether we know it or not, our relationships with our children are their first and most impactful examples of relationships, and the tempo that we set for them as they stretch themselves further out into the world is incredibly important.

Ask yourself what kind of people you hope your children surround themselves with; those who respect their ideas and beliefs, or people who discount them and tell them how to live. Think about whether you prefer your child to think about relationships as power struggles or as fertile ground for collaboration and safe exchanges of ideas. Our children learn by watching us. While we often wish they would do what we tell them to do, the fact is, they are more likely to do what we do, and they take their cues about their self-worth from the way we talk to them every day. So why wouldn't we treat them with respect and kindness? It sounds simple, but it takes practice and that is what this book is all about – offering you opportunities to practice.

Research shows that kids who don't feel as though they are listened to or taken seriously tend to do one of two things in reaction: withdraw from the relationship or ratchet up their behavior in order to get attention. Most parents can agree that both scenarios will end up causing problems, so it's important that we pay attention to our kids and help them develop positive ways of being heard. I think that the most effective way to do this is through mindfulness.

Mindfulness has been shown to increase resilience and flexibility, develop better self control, help people set safe and healthy boundaries, problem solve, address stressful situations and strengthen relationships by circumventing power struggles. Parents who nurture their children by acknowledging their needs and desires and helping them learn ways to address those needs decrease the amount of stress-related health issues for their children and have kids who do better academically. Learning to pay attention to how we are feeling and reacting to the things in our everyday lives reminds us that we have the power to choose where we focus our thoughts and energies and teaching our kids to do the same sets positive patterns in place that will serve them for the rest of their lives.

The remainder of this book uses stories to illustrate concepts, contains activities to practice on your own or with your children, and guided meditation opportunities for parents as they work through the following areas:

- Important Information About the Adolescent Brain
- Mindful Parenting
- Building Trusting Relationships
- Compassion
- Shared Goals
- Conflict
- Helping Your Child Deal with Stress & Anxiety

2 IMPORTANT INFORMATION ABOUT THE ADOLESCENT BRAIN

Adolescence is a time of rapid growth. No doubt you've noticed your grocery bill rise with your child's appetite. You've probably had to buy shoes more than once a year as your student outgrows pair after pair. You may meet your child in the kitchen before school one morning and feel as though they literally grew overnight. But what we can't see is that their brains are developing just as rapidly and significantly as their bodies are, and having some information about what's going on can help us parent them in very deliberate and effective ways.

While they may be walking and talking and performing complicated tasks (like programming the DVR or writing computer programming code at school), it turns out that much of their most important brain growth has yet to happen. There is an area of the brain called the Prefrontal Cortex (PFC) that won't be fully developed for years and years, and it is this that can make us so crazy as parents. The PFC is responsible for what are called "executive functions," including:

- the ability to reason
- solve problems creatively
- focus attention

Mind Games | What happens where in the brain

Parietal lobe
Processes touch, taste, pain, pressure, heat and cold

Frontal lobe
Coordinates speech, thought, short-term memory storage

The brain doesn't reach full maturity until at least the mid-20s. Development of brain regions and connections among them move generally from back to front areas.

Occipital lobe
Processes input from the eyes

Prefrontal cortex
Important in planning, prioritizing and complex decision-making

Back of the head

Front of the head

Cerebellum
Coordinates movement

Temporal lobe
Receives sound signals, coordinates language

Source: Massachusetts Institute of Technology

The Wall Street Journal

The image of the brain shows roughly how brain development occurs from left to right in humans. Until this area of the brain is fully mature (which is often not until around the age of 25), we are often frustrated by our teens' inability to make a rational decision. Honestly, it can often be confusing for them as well. Recognizing that these are areas our kids need to work on can help us be a little more patient with them. **Expecting an adolescent to "act like an adult" is like asking a child to swim the length of the pool at her first swim lesson.** Executive functions need to be practiced for years before they can be relied upon. The good news is that the more we practice, the better we get.

The bad news is that there is another part of the teenage brain that is hyperactive during these years – the amygdala. This is the part of the brain that is responsible for automatic emotional responses like fear and aggression. It is also associated with conditioned responses and motivation, and **the simple fact that, during adolescence, it can be swollen to nearly three times the size of an adult's amygdala means that emotions are often king in a teenager's world.** This could be part of the reason that so many teens are susceptible to anxiety, because this part of the brain is really convincing when it senses danger – even something that seems inconsequential to us, like being made fun of by their peers, can feel paralyzing to a teen. The amygdala is involved in our fear response of fight/flight/freeze and often triggers a rush of adrenaline that compels us to act or leaves us speechless. We have all seen people make choices based on pure emotion, and this is a testament to just how powerful the amygdala is.

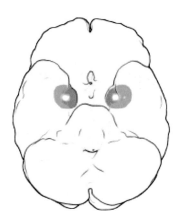

The two red areas on this picture represent the amygdala of a non-adolescent brain. In the adolescent brain, they can be up to three times their normal size, and can account for much of the high emotion during these years.

Even as adults, we can fall into the trap of wanting something so badly that we create some logical justification for getting it. Tweens and teens are very motivated by their desires and unfortunately, the portion of the brain that controls language is not the same part that controls decision-making. What that means for parents is that **we won't be able to talk our kids out of the way they feel** about something, even if we think acting on that feeling is a poor choice. What we can do is recognize how powerful their emotions are and work on redirecting them so that they use the part of their brain that controls logic. Practicing mindfulness during times of high emotion will eventually become easier for them to do on their own, but during these years of adolescence, kids can almost feel as though they are held hostage by their mood swings. It is our job to show them that they are not.

One more important thing to know about kids this age is that their brains are much more sensitive to a neurotransmitter called dopamine. Dopamine helps control the parts of the brain concerned with reward and pleasure, and during the adolescent years, we require a lot more dopamine in order to feel its effects. This means two things:

1.   Dopamine gives tweens and teens a great 'high,' and, over time,
2.   They need more and more of it to get that great feeling.

This is why kids this age tend to engage in risky behaviors. Unfortunately, when this is coupled with the inability to make rational decisions (remember their PFC isn't yet fully developed), this can mean that they act impulsively and don't stop to consider the consequences. It can also mean that they are more susceptible to becoming addicted to substances like alcohol and tobacco or illegal drugs because they trigger dopamine production and flood the brains with a potent reward. But, there are other things that trigger dopamine production as well, including pattern recognition. When we figure something out, make sense of it, our brains release dopamine. Often, even when we are simply told a story that explains a difficult concept, our brains give us a little 'high.' Stories also have been shown to prompt our brains to release oxytocin and cortisol, two hormones that decrease stress and increase our ability to connect with others.

So what do we do with this information? Can we combat it or do we just wait it out? Enter: neuroplasticity. This is a fancy scientific term that basically means we get to help shape our kids' brains. It turns out that the brain is much like any other muscle in the body – the more we work it in certain ways, the stronger it gets. So if we emphasize slowing down to let emotions dissipate before acting, thinking creatively to solve challenges, and integrating information, we can begin to build stronger pathways in the brain for those tasks. We need to use our prefrontal cortex to deal with unexpected situations, to concentrate, and to be flexible and if we do a few important things during this time of adolescence, we can make that part of our brain more efficient and functional.

So how do we set ourselves and our kids up for success? By creating an environment that makes it easier to practice these executive functions. **When we are tired, hungry, lonely, stressed or sad, we don't filter and process information as well – we tend to stay stuck in our emotions and have a hard time stepping into our PFC.** The chapters in this book address some important ways we can help our kids by modeling mindfulness and compassion, using empathy instead of shame, creating shared goals and dealing with conflict in productive ways, and teach them to deal with stress and anxiety which are a near-constant in the lives of many tweens and teens.

As parents, we are often concerned with discipline, but when our kids hit adolescence, the stakes get higher: it's not just about going to bed on time and sharing anymore. We can be plagued with thoughts of school suspensions or shoplifting charges or underage drinking. **The important thing to remember is that discipline is about learning, it isn't about revenge or even safety** (although we definitely want our kids to be safe). Adolescence is a time when we are trying to help our kids make better choices, but in order to do that, we need to make sure we are still focused on teaching them as much as we can, even if they don't seem receptive to it. Punishment is more about retribution or protecting our kids, but if we really want them to get better at looking before they leap, we have to dedicate ourselves to discipline instead of punishment. That is a tricky thing with adolescents, though, because of the unique attributes of their brains. Parenting your child while keeping in mind the challenges they have and the things they are capable of is key. They may look like little adults, and they may demand to be treated like little adults, but they aren't there yet, and remembering that during times of conflict and stress will help everyone.

3 MINDFUL PARENTING

"Our kids only know they have something to say if someone listens to them." Gloria Steinem

It may sound weird or new-agey, but mindfulness is simply the act of paying attention to what's going on in your head. The word I associate most with mindfulness is curiosity. As long as we can move to a place where we are asking questions about:

- What is happening
- How is it affecting me
- Why am I being affected like this

we are being mindful. Any time we notice that we are getting very emotional about something, whether what we are feeling is anything from anger to sadness, and we can stop for a moment before lashing out, we are being mindful. If we can stop and listen without judging or making assumptions, we are being mindful. There are many simple ways that we can practice paying attention to our children that make a big difference in their lives.

Mindful parenting can be as simple as looking up and making eye contact when your child comes into the room. It can be hard to tear ourselves away from the computer or dinner preparation or sweeping the floor or tending to another child, but acknowledging your adolescent when they walk in to the room you are in is a powerful tool. We all know what it feels like to say hello or ask someone a question and have them respond without even looking up. The message is that we aren't really important enough for them to stop what they are doing. If you can't look up or interrupt a phone conversation, at least make eye contact so they know you're acknowledging their presence.

Taking this a step further, it is vital that we examine the messages we send our kids in our habitual responses to them. Remember that every interaction during these teen years is first processed in the emotion center of your child's brain, so our words and actions are incredibly important. When you first see your child in the morning as everyone is rushing around to get ready for work and school, what do you say? Do you make a comment about their messy hair or their dirty/short/inappropriate clothing? Do you say how beautiful or handsome your child looks? Do you respond with a reminder of what time it is and how much they have left to do before they can leave? <u>All of those things are normal, and all of them are a dismissal of who your child is at their core.</u> Those messages tell them that the way the world sees them is more important than who they are. The antidote to that is to stop, make eye contact, and smile. If your child sees that you are truly happy to see them when they enter a room, they will internalize the message that they are loved.

Taking a moment to stop what you're doing and really notice your child also gives you the space to respond to them independently of what you were doing before. I call this "taking your emotional temperature."

ACTIVITY: Taking Your Emotional Temperature

We all know that when we're annoyed – stuck in traffic or paying bills or a nasty email we just got from our boss – we react to everyone and everything a little less calmly. If you're feeling rushed and frustrated when your child enters the room to ask a favor or to tell you they will be late after practice tonight, you are more likely to react negatively even if what they're saying isn't a problem. Stopping for a beat and acknowledging your frustration with the other situation and then setting it aside and shifting gears to be fully present with your child can set a different tone. That is mindful parenting.

Close your eyes and take a deep breath in and when you exhale, let the breath out through your mouth. Think about the primary emotion you're feeling right now. It might be hard to separate your emotions if you're feeling several, so just notice which ones are there.

bored   anxious   worried   restless   sad   peaceful   happy

angry   frustrated

Is there one that stands out more than the others? Try not to get caught up in the story behind the emotions or explain why or try to figure it out. Just note what you're feeling more than anything else. If there is one word that stands out more than another, focus on it and see if you can feel where that affects your body. If you're angry or frustrated, maybe it shows up as a tightness in your chest. If you're happy, maybe there's a warm glow in your belly. Don't think about why you feel the way you do or judge whether it's good or bad, just notice.

When you're ready, take a deep breath and open your eyes. Write down the top two or three emotions you're feeling in this moment. That is your emotional temperature. At any given time, you are feeling a collection of different things, but there are always one or two that are more prevalent than the others.

Why does your emotional temperature matter? Because our brains work so quickly to react to situations we are in that, depending on the temperature, we will say and do different things.

Think about how slowly things move when it's cold. Imagine your thoughts and words as honey. When your emotional temperature is cool (peaceful, joyful, happy) you are more likely to react to a new or unexpected situation with curiosity and optimism. It is as if you are wearing rose-colored glasses that see everything as glass-half-full. You are less likely to jump to conclusions.

When it's warm, honey runs quickly. If you are feeling anxious or fearful, angry or frustrated, you are more likely to assume bad intent or negative outcomes. Your reactions are swift and decisive, as if you're wearing dark glasses that see shadow instead of light.

Whenever your kids come to you with a challenge or request, take a second to get your emotional temperature. So often, the other things that are going on around us lead us to react in ways that are inappropriate or disproportionate to the situation. When we are grieving, we tend to be more irritable or quick to anger. When we are tired or anxious, we respond negatively to others. Recognizing your emotional temperature at any given time is a way to remember that even if we are having a stressful day, we can choose to respond to our children in a different way without taking it out on them.

Mindful parenting is also being careful with the words we use in reference to our kids.

Our brains are obsessed with shortcuts – we use them all the time. We create nicknames and labels for people so that we can generalize and make decisions more quickly. A lot of the time that doesn't hurt anything, but when it comes to our kids, it can mean that we aren't connecting with them or we are making assumptions about their motivations or desires that aren't true. By the time they hit adolescence, we have had years and years to form opinions about who our kids are and what makes them tick. Unfortunately, adolescence is a time where our kids are stretching themselves and trying on new identities and they may not want to be put in those little tiny boxes anymore, so it's important to examine the things we think we know about our kids. Even if we think we are letting them explore some new ways to interact with the world, we often don't give them as much freedom to do so at home. We make assumptions based on who we "know" they are (the oldest is the 'clever, crafty one' and the youngest kid is the 'kamikaze who doesn't look before he leaps') and we often react to them from that place without thinking.

ACTIVITY: Labels

What if we step back and challenge those ideas a little bit? We could send a message of tolerance and curiosity about our kids instead of boxing them in to a place where they might not be happy. Here are four questions you can ask yourself the next time you jump to conclusions about your child's motives or beliefs.:

1. What assumption am I making about my child right now and is it true?
    At this point, it is easy for our brains to start rationalizing by listing supporting evidence for our assumptions. "Of course he's the kamikaze! Look how many broken bones he has had. Remember the time he moved all his furniture around and broke the bookcase?"
2. Are there other instances I can think of that counteract this label I've given my kid?
    Could it be that he's really athletic and determined to give 110% and that accounts for the broken bones? Are there times when he has done something risky and pulled it off brilliantly? Can I think of other times when he has been appropriately cautious? What if I think about the other side of the 'kamikaze' coin as 'courage?'
3. What is my gut reaction to the assumption I'm making about my child?
    Am I disgusted because he's nothing like me or am I frightened because that is exactly how I acted at that age and it got me into trouble? What is my deep emotional response to him and could that have something to do with how I treat him when he makes a mistake?
4. What happens if I let go of that label and try to see my child as a person with many different attributes and abilities?
    How might he respond if I let go of the label and see him through a different lens? How might my reaction to him be different the next time he comes to me with a problem? Would our interaction be more satisfying if I simply asked questions about why he makes the choices he makes instead of acting on an assumption?

Some common labels we use for other people include:

Perfectionist	Scaredy-cat	Control freak	Introvert
Extrovert	Kamikaze	Fearless	Scattered
Airhead	Jock	Princess	Show-off

There may be ample evidence of one or more of those labels, but if we think we 'know' our kids, we trick ourselves into making assumptions about their motives and their future. We can end up setting expectations for them that they don't feel like they can escape. We stop listening to them and they stop talking to us. If we give them the freedom to try out new attitudes and interests, we can encourage them to break free of rigid stereotypes and let them know that we think they are capable of many different things.

The Myth of Multitasking

We are asked to do it all the time. Job postings ask for candidates that are "good multitaskers," smartphones and computer software advertise their ability to multitask, we are told that women are better at it than men because they often juggle so many different things at once. But the fact is, our brains are not able to multitask at all, they just switch rapidly back and forth between different thoughts and jobs and it happens so quickly that we don't even notice it. *'What's wrong with that?'* you're thinking. Often, there isn't anything wrong with that. But sometimes this quick swapping gets us into trouble by leading us to believe things that aren't true.

I have a big dog and I walk him several times a day. One day I was walking him and he stopped to relieve himself in the grass alongside the street. I pulled a bag out of my pocket and bent over to clean it up just as he saw another dog coming our way and started to tug on the leash. That slight tug led me to look up from what I was doing and slightly shift my left foot. As I looked down the street, the toes of my foot came down on something about an inch in diameter and I panicked, thinking that I was stepping in the dog poop. I jumped back, nearly falling on my butt on the sidewalk, and let out a gasp. That's all I needed – poop on my shoe! I was instantly annoyed with the dog and yanked his leash back toward me. When I turned my attention back to the grass, I saw that I had stepped on a piece of a branch that had fallen from the tree above me and I felt silly. But it was the perfect illustration of how our mind connects the dots for us without having all the information. Because I had been poised to clean up my dog's mess, when I stepped on something that was slightly similar (although much harder and not in the exact area), my brain completed the picture, initiated the fear response, and I got mad at my dog for his friendly response to the other dog coming our way. It made me wonder how often I do that to my kids. If I have just heard about some social difficulty going on at my daughter's school from another parent and my daughter gets into the car saying she has had a bad day, it feels normal for me to assume that I know why. But I could be really wrong, and it doesn't hurt to ask her before launching into my version of things.

This is where I can use mindful parenting tactics. Being aware of the fact that my brain has a tendency to fill in the gaps of knowledge without me even trying means that I have to check my assumptions all the time. Even if I think I know what's going on, what is motivating my kid, where they're coming from, I need to step back, breathe, and remind myself that I might just be making stuff up. Asking questions, remaining curious, and recognizing my limitations are all components of mindful parenting that can keep us from making hasty decisions that might cause conflict with our kids.

Modeling An Empowered View of Life

So much of parenting is modeling. Our children watch us and, whether they know it or not, many of their standard reactions to life events come about because of the way we react. Ask yourself how you react when things don't turn out the way you want them to. Do you blame someone else? Do you scold yourself? Do you say, *'I don't deserve this!'* or lament your bad luck? Those are all examples of disempowerment, of living life as though it happens to you, feeling at the whim of fate or luck. If our children see us as people who don't have much say over what happens in life, they will begin to believe that and act that way, too. If they watch us judge and label every experience and take things personally, they think that that is how life is. If they hear us say that we value certain things, but then watch us go through our day in a very different way, they will come to understand that what we say we value isn't really all that important. Everyone struggles and has challenges and deals with unexpected events on a daily basis, but how we handle those things makes all the difference. It is important to teach our children to experience life without feeling powerless and without needing to change it.

ACTIVITY: When Things Don't Go Your Way

1. Acknowledge your feelings (*I'm angry or frustrated. I'm nervous or sad*)

2. Acknowledge the situation and the fact that it can't be changed right now (*We are stuck in traffic. Dinner is burned. My wallet got stolen.*)

3. Try to resist judging the feelings (*I shouldn't feel this way* or *Why can't I let go of this?*) or making up stories about them (*If only I hadn't... Because of her, ...*) **This is the hardest part and it takes practice.** So many of us barely pay attention to the actual feeling and make the leap right to justifying or explaining it or creating scenarios in our head about what could happen as a result. But part of feeling empowered is letting our feelings arise and recede. If we don't fight them or exaggerate them with stories in our heads, they will last about 90 seconds and subside. Doing step 1 and 2 and then stopping for a couple of minutes can often interrupt our anxiety reactions

4. Decide what your most important value is in regard to the situation and find a way to get there. (*If you are going to be late for an important appointment but you're stuck in traffic, can you call the person who is waiting for you and see if they have an alternative? If dinner is burned and you need to feed the family, can you all agree to have peanut butter sandwiches tonight and try again tomorrow?*)

4 TRUSTING RELATIONSHIPS

Shame and Empathy

"There's a difference between saying, 'why do you think you did that?' and saying, 'how could you do that?' which is not a question but an accusation. Which is another way of saying, 'you have forfeited your right to be understood. Shame on you.'" Gregory Martin

Shame is an emotion that shuts down pathways to learning in the brain. It is also a destructive emotion that has the effect of isolating us from others. Dr. Brené Brown, a researcher at the University of Houston, has done a lot of work with shame and guilt and talks about the difference between the two as a simple but important distinction. **Guilt comes about when we acknowledge that we have done something wrong. Shame is what happens to us when we personalize our actions and let them define us** – it's the difference between saying, "I am a bad person" and saying, "I did a bad thing." Shame tells us that there is something basically flawed inside us and it doesn't give us a way back. Guilt makes us think about what we have done and how to atone for it, but it doesn't mean that we are doomed to make the same mistakes over and over again. This is why the language we use with our kids is so important. If we accuse them of lying, that is one bad act. If we call them a liar, that means we see them as someone who has that as a personality trait. Someone who has heard themselves called a liar enough times will begin to internalize that message and live that way.

As a kid, I was often shamed by my parents who saw it as a great way to keep me in line, to ensure that I acted the way they wanted me to. What I learned from that was that the most important thing was that I do the "Right" thing, what I didn't learn was how to determine what the "Right" thing is without asking my parents. The most recent research shows that shame is pretty effective at changing short-term behavior, but it doesn't ultimately change their values or emotions. That is important to understand because someone who is only acting a certain way because they are either afraid of how you see them or of getting punished will eventually stop trying to be in relationship with you. Over time, they will either stop engaging with you, get really good at hiding their behavior from you, or increase the intensity of their negative behavior in order to get you to pay attention. None of these things is what we ultimately want for our children. What we really want is for them to be in relationship with us and to learn from their mistakes. Shaming teaches them that they ARE their mistakes and keeps them from learning much of anything else. Shaming our kids is the same as rejecting them which is particularly painful coming from someone who is supposed to love you unconditionally.

Empathy is the opposite of shame.

Having empathy for our kids means that we can walk a mile in their shoes – we can see things from their perspective. **It is important to note that even though you have empathy for someone, you aren't excusing their behavior.** I remember doing some pretty stupid things when I was a teenager and I am thrilled that none of those things are seen as the entire story of who I am and what I could become. If I can remember this when my kids mess up, I can begin to have some kindness in my heart for them, even if I am angry or frustrated or fearful of the consequences they might reap from their actions. Finding empathy is the beginning of separating my reactions from their behavior and it can help them to begin to sort out their own solutions to the mess they find themselves in. Once I've set aside my emotions, I can ask "why do you think you did that?" The purpose of this question is to give them an opportunity to have some self-awareness, to start to understand both how things like this happen and whether they were acting in accordance with their own values at the time. They may not be able to answer you, but at least you've given them the chance to begin thinking about why they make the choices they make, and remember, it's all about practice.

Trust
"Trust is an outcome of honest conversation, not a prerequisite for it."

We know that trust is an important component of a good relationship, but we don't always know how to go about creating it. One of the first things that has to be present for there to be trust is a feeling of safety. If I know that I can say what I truly feel without being attacked or made fun of, I am more likely to be honest, and the more honest I am, the more likely the other person is to be honest with me. Another piece of a trusting relationship involves knowing that the other party wants to know what is important to me. And the best way to get that knowledge is to ask. When we are curious about our children, we let them know that their thoughts and values are important to us. Asking lots of questions is a great way to get to know what makes them tick. What do they value? Why do they choose some of the things they do? How do they see the world and their place in it? These kinds of questions all validate their right to have an opinion, even if it isn't exactly the same as yours, and it gives them an opportunity to identify what they want from life and to practice speaking up about it.

ACTIVITY: Trust-building

The following exercise was created by Kim Bogucki, founder of The IF Project, in an attempt to build bridges between prison inmates and police officers – two communities that historically don't trust each other at all. Sit down with your child one night and have them answer these three questions on a sheet of paper. At the same time, answer them yourself and when you're done, talk about the things you've written down.

- What is one belief or perception I have about you?
- What is one thing you don't know about me?
- What would make our interaction easier for me?

It may seem simple, but often the answers to the first two questions can be pretty surprising. The last question offers you both the chance to define your own boundaries and be creative about how you can maintain or strengthen your relationship with your child.

Making mistakes:

We know that kids this age make decisions based on emotions, even if they are attempting to rationalize them to themselves or us. In fact, we all make emotional decisions and then use logic to justify those choices, often without even realizing it. So when your teen makes a decision for some reason known only to them (I blew my entire allowance on that music download because I'm the only one who doesn't know all the words to those songs and I need to fit in or I feel stupid), you won't be able to talk them out of the emotion behind it. The best you can do is understand the emotion (fitting in is really important to me and being socially isolated is scary) and help them understand that that is what drives them, too. Then, you might be able to help them define some other values they have (saving money for college, helping pay for their phone bill to stay connected to friends) and strategize about ways to achieve the same goal (learning the words to the songs) without that particular risk. When you bring the "why" out in to the light, you are helping them think about whether things they think are important really ought to be. The trick is to not inject *your* values into the conversation, because, again, you will never be able to talk them out of feeling the way they feel, and sending them the message that their feelings are somehow wrong will only keep them from being honest with you. The goal of this particular phase of life is to learn to make good choices, but we have to make them in accordance with our own beliefs and value systems, so the best (and likely, most frustrating) thing you can do is help them identify their own goals and decide whether their actions are in line with those goals.

PARENTING TIP: Shorthand for Teens and Tweens

When my oldest daughter was in the 6th grade, we lived about 45 minutes' drive from her school. This gave us ample time to both prepare for and debrief from her days in middle school. We had several other girls in our carpool for the first twenty minutes of the drive and I loved listening to them talk about classwork and teachers and social dynamics. From time to time, after everyone else was gone, my daughter would sigh and prepare to complain about something that was bothering her. In the beginning, like most parents, my instinct was to fix it. I assumed that she was telling me because she wanted my insight and often, I would interrupt her to tell some story from my life that was similar (I thought). Not surprisingly, she often got frustrated with me – both for interrupting and for making it about me. After a few incidents like this, I realized that she might soon stop talking to me about things like this altogether.

Ironically, I assumed from the beginning that she was telling me these things because she trusted me, and she probably was, but she was shutting down and getting angry because I wasn't returning that level of trust. By interrupting and giving her advice every single time, I was letting her know that I didn't trust her to handle the situation herself, or to think creatively about it at all. I was simply giving her the answer. My answer. So I created a shorthand. When she told me about something that had upset her, before saying anything else, I asked her this: "What do you need from me right now? Is this venting, do you want my opinion, or are you asking for my advice?"

More often than not, she was simply venting and if she said so, it gave me permission to relax and just listen. Nothing more was required of me than to be a friendly ear. I didn't have to get caught up in the emotion or rush to think of any solutions. She just needed to release her frustrations and move on.

From time to time, as she wound down, she would change her mind and ask me for my (short) opinion. Very occasionally she asked for my advice. But the most important thing about this shorthand was that it gave her control and it let me know what was expected of me. She would often hear herself talking and come up with her own solution to the issue – and generally it was one that I never would have created. At the times when she was simply venting, I was reinforcing the message that sometimes what we really need to do is let go of the things we can't control and move on.

5 COMPASSION

It is sometimes hard to have compassion for our teens, especially when we are filled with fear for their safety or afraid that we have messed up somewhere along the way and have turned them into horrible people. So often, we assume that we know what motivates them (greed, narcissism, selfishness, simply not thinking) and we react accordingly. But compassion is necessary for good, strong relationships. Being willing to spend some time in the other person's shoes and proactively working to make things better is important for connection. Sometimes, with our children, what we are reacting to is the knowledge of *what we were like as teens.* But remaining curious about our kids and why they make the choices they do is the first step in acting compassionately toward them. This means stopping short of assuming anything which is tremendously difficult, but it gets easier with practice.

"Where there is bad behavior, there is pain."

My youngest daughter gets overwhelmed by certain situations with lots of sensory input. She hates the volume in a movie theater. She gets paralyzed by the sights and sounds and smells and people offering her samples at Costco. She is very particular about the kind of clothing she wears, hates tags of any kind, and can be a bit obsessive about making things "even."

Over the years she has taught herself ways to accommodate and/or avoid things that make her a little nuts and in many cases, as she gets older, she challenges herself to endure some very difficult situations in order to practice desensitizing herself. She has come a very long way in learning to tolerate things that were once unthinkable, but a few sticking points remain. She is terribly susceptible to motion sickness and she struggles with transitions. The first few weeks of summer are really rough, as are the first few weeks of school after a carefree summer. We generally have a few days of teeth-grinding frustration before she settles into the new phase, but I've learned to steel myself for it every year.

One year, we decided to surprise our girls with a trip on their mid-winter break from school. We live in a pretty dark, rainy climate and decided that we needed to go find the sunshine. We orchestrated everything without any suspicion on their part until the night before when we gave them each a packing list complete with shorts and swimsuits. They were thrilled.

I didn't even consider what this might be like for my youngest child. By the third day, she was on edge. She had spent two full days jettisoning herself between the beach and the pool, lying in the sun reading and going for walks with her older sister while her father and I relaxed and had adult conversations. Until Day Three.

As is their ritual, my husband and my oldest daughter got up before sunrise to go for a beach walk and coffee. My youngest and I lazily made our way into our swimsuits and promised to join them shortly. As soon as they left the hotel room, Lauren complained that her hair was sticking up and dropped the hairbrush on the tile floor. I rolled my eyes, dropped the beach bag and wet a washcloth thoroughly to plaster it down.

"As soon as it dries, it's gonna stick up all over again!" she yelled. I shushed her, worried that she would wake our hotel neighbors. She stomped her foot and glared at me.

Then the strings on her swimsuit bottom made "uncomfortable lumps" beneath her shorts and she tugged and fussed and picked at it as enormous tears formed in her eyes. I was ready to go and wanted coffee. She was being ridiculous. I told her to figure it out.

Next, she couldn't get her flip flops to go on smoothly and caught one of them in her toe and flung it across the room, smacking it against the picture hanging on the wall. I was furious and about two inches from grabbing her by the arm as I shushed her again, warning her not to wake anyone else up.

"I DON'T CARE ABOUT THE NEIGHBORS!!" she shouted and I found myself at a crossroads. Mentally cataloguing the morning's catastrophes – from itchy, sandy shoes to hair disasters to sunburned shoulders to this, I suddenly stopped.

Where there is bad behavior, there is pain.

This had all the earmarks of a classic transition meltdown. Each of those petty things would normally not phase her. She wasn't trying to be difficult. She was hurting. I put down my bag again and joined her on the bed where she lie face down, sobbing with spine-shaking gulps.

"I think that this might be what it looks like to be uncomfortable in your own skin. Do you think so?" I kissed the top of her head as she nodded emphatically.

"I – I – I don't know what to doooooo," she wailed pathetically and my heart broke open a little. I had to help her.

"I'm sorry we sprung this trip on you and I know you're trying to enjoy it. Do you think we can find a way to help you settle in a little bit and start to feel more in control of things?" I led her through some deep breathing exercises and a quick guided meditation and then when she was calm, we sat and talked about what she wanted to be in charge of. She didn't get punished for her behavior. Instead, I taught her how to begin to recognize when she is feeling out of control and brainstormed ways for her to let someone know that she needs help before it gets too big. She felt like I was on her side at the end of our conversation instead of being angry with me for forcing her to "get over it" or punishing her for feeling the way she felt. The rest of our vacation was pretty terrific, and since then, it hasn't taken much reminding to get her to anticipate when things might get tough and ask for help instead of acting out.

ACTIVITY: Ask yourself first

One way to begin thinking about how to relate to your child with compassion is to define for yourself what you need when you're struggling. It sounds simple, but we don't often react in ways that we would like to be treated. Remember a time when you were really struggling with something and answer these questions:

- What do I need to hear when I'm struggling? *I need to hear that it isn't my fault. I need to hear that someone loves me and supports me no matter what. I need to know that I'm not alone.*
- When I pour my heart out to someone, what do I want them to do most? *I might think I want them to*

'fix' it, but ultimately, what I really want is a hug or to have them just sit with me while I grieve.

The next thing to do is to ask your child what he or she needs when they are struggling. Not everyone wants or needs the same things, and it's important that we don't react to our kids in ways that shut down the communication. Often, there are similar themes in what we want, and that can be a great way to start a conversation with your adolescent.

<u>The Opposite of What You Know is Also True</u>

This is a lesson we share with kids in the SELF Project curriculum, but it is just as applicable for parents. During a TED talk, Derek Sivers told a story about traveling in Japan. He was looking for a particular place and stopped someone to ask for the address. The person he asked gave him the name of a block in the city, but he was confused. He tried to clarify and asked for the street name. The man answered, "The streets don't have names. Streets are simply the empty space between blocks. The blocks have names."

He was confused. Clearly there was some language barrier. He tried again, and the man asked, "What is the name of the block you live on?"

Derek replied, "The blocks don't have names. The streets have names. The blocks are simply the empty spaces between streets."

In some villages in China, the local physician is paid on a daily basis by the townspeople. He comes by each house in the morning to collect his coins from a box placed outside for that purpose. If he happens upon one house where there is no money put outside for him, he knows there is someone inside who is sick and his services are needed. In these villages, the physician is only paid when the people in his care are healthy. They believe that this is the best way to ensure that everyone stays healthy, or at least does their best to prevent getting sick.

It is impossible for our brains to hold two opposing ideas simultaneously. Consider this famous drawing of the old lady/young lady by WE Hill:

Some people will immediately see an old woman with a bonnet on, her chin tucked into her collar.

Others will see a young woman with her head turned away in profile, only the tip of her nose and her eyelash visible.

You can't see both of them at the same time, but your brain can flip back and forth between the two. Consider how, when we are caught up in our own ideas and stories about what our kids are doing, we are literally unable to consider another option. But if we can cultivate the ability to let go of our assumptions, and remember that the opposite of what we "know" is also true – just from a different perspective – we can be compassionate and understanding and perhaps avoid a conflict.

<u>Barriers to Kindness</u>

There are a lot of experts that say that parenting isn't about being your child's friend. Many of us were parented with a "tough love" philosophy that held us accountable for everything and strove to build us into strong, independent adults who could handle all sorts of difficult situations alone. But the truth is, human beings are rarely completely on their own. At work, we are expected to collaborate and help one another. At home, if we live with others, we need to know how to cooperate and support each others' needs. In our marriages and committed relationships, we don't act as two separate, independent adults. We are interdependent, and while it is important to be able and willing to take responsibility for our actions and choices, it is equally as important to know our own personal limitations and be able to find people to rely on when we need it most.

It is tempting, as a parent, to think that once our children reach high school, they need to practice cleaning up all of their own messes. There are many school teachers and administrators that will advise you to back off and let your children fail in order to help them learn. And while it is important for teens to develop resilience and responsibility, that doesn't mean that we can't offer them emotional support and kindness when they do make mistakes. Sometimes it is hard to watch our children struggle and I know I've been guilty of pretending that I am indifferent to their suffering just so they aren't tempted to rely on me too much. But I'm not sure that sends the message I really want to send. Ultimately, I hope that my children will come to me for emotional support and, if they really find themselves in trouble, I want them to know that there are adults in their lives who can help them brainstorm solutions. When our kids are feeling low for whatever reason, it is never wrong to show them kindness, regardless of how they got to that point, but it is easy to fall prey to some of the myths about kindness:

1. *I don't have anything to offer.* Sometimes, we feel like being kind to someone means giving them an out, or coming up with a solution for their problem. In all honesty, though, we always have kindness to offer to our children, and it's amazing how far a hug or a smile or a pat on the back will go toward letting our kids know we're in their corner.

2. *I'll look weak.* When you're angry with your child (especially if they've done something you cautioned against and ended up getting in trouble), it's tempting to stick to your guns, punish them or say 'I told you so,' and hold fast. We think we will look like we're caving in if we commiserate, but that's not the case. It is possible to empathize with their situation (*"Ouch, that must have hurt,"* or *"I'm sorry you're feeling so bad right now,"*) and still uphold your family rules or enforce consequences for their behavior.

3. *I'll get taken advantage of.* This is really a variation on the previous barrier. But if you show kindness and still manage to enforce rules, you will have shown your child that you care for them **and** they are responsible for their own choices. There's nothing to take advantage of in that scenario.

4. *I'm too angry/too sad to be nice right now.* This is a tricky one, but as the adult in the relationship, it's a great lesson for our kids. Being overwhelmed with emotion is never a good reason not to do the right thing, and we know that no matter how angry we are with someone, we can still love and care for them. Being able to express both your immediate feelings and your over-arching connection to your child simultaneously reminds them that your love for them is unconditional and it gives them some insight into how their behavior affects other people. I have been known to say to my

daughters, "I am so hurt by your choices right now and I want you to know that I love you and I hope you are able to make this right."

"Forgiveness means giving up all hope for a better past." Lily Tomlin

I love this quote because it reminds me that what is done is done and my job is to move forward and make the days to come better. My relationship with my children will last for years to come and if I can't forgive them for the mistakes they make as children, I won't be able to forge a strong bond with them.

6 SHARED GOALS

It may seem obvious when our children are young that we all share similar goals. We want them to be healthy, happy, and find purpose in their lives. But as they get older and begin making more choices about their own lives, it can feel as though we don't really want the same things anymore. Remember, it is their job to become individuals, to find their own passions and talents, and this task can cause tension in the home if you don't agree with what is important to them. While it may not be possible for everyone to come to consensus on everything, talking with your child about their values and goals is a good way for you to understand each other and find some common ground.

ACTIVITY: Four Questions

1. *What is your parenting style?* This is not a question that should cause you to judge yourself, it is merely designed to shine a light on how you interact with your children. Do you tend to leave them to their own devices most of the time and then occasionally really hone in on things? For a variety of reasons, many parents let their kids be fairly autonomous until there is a problem (grades slip or they get caught shoplifting) and then they pay very close attention or come down hard with punishment. Maybe you are the kind of parent who values peace and kindness above all and prefers to be friends with your child. Other types of parents include those who act out of fear (lots of rules, restrictions, supervision), those who demand respect (children should be seen and not heard, my way or the highway), and those who are consistent but middle-of-the road when it comes to authority. Again, this exercise is not about "good" or "bad" parenting styles, it is simply about being aware of how you've chosen to parent. Because the next question to ask is…

2. *What is your child's style?* Are they defiant or compliant? Do they react strongly and loudly when things go wrong or are they fairly stoic? Is your child volatile or go-with-the-flow? Do they rely on you for advice and life skills or are they very independent? Are they withdrawn at home or social and right in the thick of things? Take a minute and look at your parenting style next to your child's style. No judgment, just observation. If you are a parent who wants to be your child's friend but they are withdrawn at home, that might give you some information about what kinds of things might set you both off.

3. *What is your overall parenting goal?* When you think about what you want your parenting life to have been all about, is it a peaceful home or a healthy child? Is it that your child grows up to be financially successful or quiet and respectful of others? Do you hope that you have a close emotional relationship with your child or is it more important to you that they leave home one day and don't rely on you for help (emotional or otherwise)? What do you see your 'job' as a parent being – to raise a productive individual or just to keep your child safe until they graduate from high school? Think about all of the things you most want out of your parenting life.

4. *What are the barriers to those parenting goals?* Keeping in mind your style, your child's style and your goals, are there things you can see that stand in the way?

19

Growth versus Fixed Mindset

Carol Dweck is a professor of psychology at Stanford University and she has written a great deal about something she calls 'mindset' and how it affects our ability to be resilient and deal with challenges. Her ideas are based on the notion that there are two different mindsets – fixed and growth. The Fixed Mindset says that people are born with a particular level of intelligence that they'll have forever. When we hear people say things like "he is just good at math but I'm not" or "no matter how much I study, I'm still going to flunk this test," those comments indicate that they have a fixed mindset.

The Growth Mindset is one that leads us to believe that hard work and effort are just as important as intelligence. People who believe in their ability to get better by practicing and challenging themselves have a growth mindset. These people tend to be happier and more able to bounce back from disappointment because they see obstacles as ways to get better.

Interestingly, we tend to have a growth mindset when it comes to our children, but not necessarily when it comes to ourselves. We encourage our kids to work hard, to practice piano or free throws or times tables, but some of us think that we have reached our own capacity to learn, and we often give up when we face large challenges or harsh criticism. Modeling a growth mindset for our kids can help them understand that no matter our age or place in life, we are always capable of improving ourselves and learning new things. When our children embrace the idea that they can continue to get better by working hard, they will feel empowered and motivated to learn. Following is an activity that can help you identify which kind of mindset you use with your adolescent.

ACTIVITY: Growth v. Fixed Mindset

1. Notice what kinds of things you praise your child for. Is it hard work and effort or is it grades? Do you celebrate when their team wins a game or when you see them improving after every practice?

2. Listen to what you're thinking when your child struggles with something. Does that voice in your head say, *'She just can't memorize things'* or *'Wow, she's working really hard. I wonder if there is another approach she can take to understand this?'*

3. Think about how you can point your child to opportunities for growth. Can you look at their report card and ask if there is someone who can help tutor them or a teacher they trust? Do they have an older sibling that can walk them through a difficult concept? Are you more concerned about punishing them for mistakes than helping them do better next time?

4. Listen to what you're thinking when your child triumphs and how you point out what led to that. Do you say, *'You are such a natural athlete!'* or *'I'm proud of how hard you've been working to perfect that shot. It obviously worked!'*

5. Listen to the things your child says about their triumphs and struggles. Are there things they have given up on because they think they aren't good at them? Do they value their own hard work as much as the outcome they get?

ACTIVITY: Values Worksheet

Part of having shared goals with someone else is understanding what is truly important to them. The following questions are a great way to get some insight into your child's emotional life and the things that drive them. Sharing your answers with them and reading their responses can go a long way toward understanding why we make the choices we make.

1. What are your favorite things to do?

2. Who are your favorite people? Why?

3. If you had to choose between two events, how would you decide?

4. What is your default emotion?

5. What sorts of things make you terribly angry?

6. What sorts of things make you terribly sad?

7. What sorts of things make you immeasurably happy?

8. What could you do without for the rest of your life?

9. What are you most afraid of losing in your life?

Your child may not feel comfortable answering all of these questions (and you might not, either), but even doing a few of them opens up a conversation that can lead to a deeper view of who we are and what we truly care about. You can answer them all at once, like a worksheet, or ask one or two a day at a meal or in the car.

ACTIVITY: Highs and Lows

This is something you and your family can do once a week. It's fairly low-key and as long as everyone sticks to the guidelines, it's simple and serves to give everyone insight into others' lives and offers each family member an opportunity to share something about themselves. You can do it in the car on the way to school or church or sitting around the dinner table or anytime you're all together for 15 minutes or so. Make sure everyone gets a turn to share their highest and lowest moments or experiences of the last week. Talking about both is a great way to remind us that life is neither all good or all bad. The trick to making sure this goes smoothly and leaves everyone feeling okay is to follow the rules below:

1. <u>No taking anything personally.</u> This isn't about you (even if your son says his low point was the fight the two of you got in last Tuesday). This is a time for each person to share an experience that laid them low and that's all. If everyone vows not to take anything personally, the others will feel as though they can be totally honest.

2. <u>No making things personal.</u> Your low point has to be about you – use "I" statements. Calling someone else out for something they said or did isn't fair, especially if it happened a few days ago. You can absolutely say that your low point came about when you felt really sad that there was an argument about laundry, but please don't say something like, "When Markus left his dirty clothes on the floor for everyone to trip over."

3. <u>No fixing.</u> It is really tempting to offer advice when someone talks about being upset or sad. Now is

not the time. This is just about sharing our experiences and getting some perspective on our own lives and the lives of our loved ones.

4.   <u>No judgment.</u> It is also tempting to compare our low points to others' (mine was way worse than yours) or somehow express that we think someone else is taking something too seriously. We don't get to judge how someone reacts emotionally to any situation. What might be hard for them could be something that doesn't phase us at all, and that's okay. Please don't belittle someone else's lows or highs just because you would have reacted differently.

5.   <u>End with the highs.</u> This is a great reminder that we can choose how we see the world every single day. And leaving with the highs fresh in our mind is likely to give us a boost that will last for a while.

ACTIVITY: Appreciation Board

I am always looking for ways to re-frame the way we think about each other in our house. When everyone is in a hurry, stressed about homework and quizzes, their place on the team and getting dinner on the table, it can be hard to remember what we like about each other. Instead, we tend to focus on how other people in the house are getting in our way. One antidote to this is the Appreciation Board. All it takes is a chalkboard, whiteboard, or large sheet of paper in the kitchen. Write everyone's names at the top of the board with the beginning of a sentence beneath it like this:

You can start things by quietly circling one person's name and finishing the sentence. When I did it, everyone was still asleep and they came downstairs for breakfast and the board read, "Eve is so awesome because … she is such a good friend to her friends." Some kids will acknowledge it loudly, and others will be quiet and calm about it, but it always feels good to be called out for something special about you. Here are the rules for the Appreciation Board in our house:

1. It can be (but doesn't have to be) anonymous
2. Each message gets to stay up for a minimum of three days
3. Only positive, supportive messages will be left visible
4. Messages that reflect someone's best qualities are preferred (as opposed to an act they performed)

I love this simple way of reminding our kids that looking for something positive about others is important and powerful. So often our communication at home centers around things we need done or small conflicts we have, but shining a light on the things we take for granted about each other is a great way to build family unity.

7 CONFLICT

If you have children, at some point you will have conflict. We don't always agree on how or when to do things, and there are many times when we think we know what is going on, but we really don't. Add in the emotional volatility of a teenager, and things can get ugly. While we can't avoid all conflict in our lives, we can get better at addressing it and maintaining our integrity and our relationships. Ironically, it's not even really a good thing to avoid conflict, because that generally means we aren't willing to connect with others. Even if it is uncomfortable for us, it is important to learn how to have conversations where we disagree with others respectfully, because that is how we learn.

Generally, conflict is about power – who has it and who wants it. If we don't care about the outcome, we don't care about fighting for it, but if we want something, or believe we deserve something, we will go to the mat. The trick as a parent is to determine who wants what and try to understand why, rather than asserting our power over our children. When power struggles start, often we end up setting aside the real issue in favor of winning. [Erin Twilight story here] I have learned that as kids get older, they get more clever at finding ways to get what they want and if I forbid them from something, they are more likely to lie to me or sneak around and get it anyway than they are to simply bow to my authority.

Going Beyond "No"

When my oldest daughter was in 4th grade, the Twilight books were very popular. Erin was in school with several girls who had older sisters and many of them had read the book. We were knee-deep in the Harry Potter series at that time, and I was feeling good about my daughter's enthusiasm for reading. One day, she came home from school and asked me if she could read the first Twilight book. I was a little scared because I felt like those books were too mature for her at the time, but she was really working hard to make her case. She told me about all of her friends who had read them, about the one whose older sister had them all and would loan them to her for as long as she needed, and she said that they even had them in the school library.

I had a choice to make. I knew that if I said no, there was a chance she would find a way to get them anyway. The school librarian had a policy of letting any student check out any book as a way to encourage reading for pleasure. I also knew that my stubborn, independent child would continue to work me until I said yes. I put her off for a few days while I thought about it and eventually made her a deal. We would read the first book together, book-club style. This would allow me to have a conversation with her every couple of chapters so that we could discuss some of the more mature themes in the book. While I wasn't excited at all about reading this book, it was the only way I felt like I could maintain an understanding of what it is she wanted to get out of it and inject some of my parental values into the mix. She agreed.

She lasted about five chapters. The more we read together, the more she realized that it wasn't her kind of book. Much of the romantic aspects flew right over her head (thank goodness), and the rest was so poorly written (as compared to Harry Potter) that she couldn't stand it. The more we talked about it, the more she opened up about her true reason for wanting to read the series, which was to be able to talk to her friends about it and 'fit in.' Ultimately, she decided it wasn't worth it to slog through a book that she didn't enjoy and she chose to abandon it in favor of finding other activities she could do with her friends. Putting aside my desire to wield authority over her by saying no, I was able to connect with her in a way that allowed her some freedom but held her to an examination of her motivation and her values. Had I said no, I'm certain she would have just found a way to read it, anyway, and while she may have still given up on the books, there would certainly have been conflict around her defying me.

There are different types of conflict, to be sure. The easiest ones to handle are the ones that aren't blowing up in my face – the request to go to a party next weekend or to watch a particular TV show that I don't think my child is ready for. I have taught my kids over the years that I need time to make those kinds of decisions and that they can't expect me to answer right away. Buying myself time lets me acknowledge my initial gut reaction and then ask questions about why I think I reacted that way.

Conflict is rooted in emotion and when the emotion centers of our brain are in full-play, we immediately go into a fight/flight/fear response. As we know from adolescent brain development, during the t(w)een years, this response is exaggerated, so when we enter into conflict with our children without defusing the emotional response, we are setting ourselves up for trouble. **When emotions are high, the portion of the brain that learns is shut down, so when conflict is about winning, it can't be about learning.** Not only do we need to defuse the bomb of our own emotions, but we have to wait for our kids to do the same. When one person is calm and rational and the other is emotionally fired up, there can be no connection and no dialogue. That doesn't mean that the emotional response is wrong or inappropriate, but conversation and resolution can't happen until the emotion is acknowledged and dealt with. I know that I have never done or said anything out of extreme anger that I felt good about later.

ACTIVITY: Defusing Anger

When volatile situations come up, try to go through the following steps with your child so that you can both take a minute to process your strong feelings and move on to a place where you can talk constructively.

- recognize the signs of anger *(chest tight, heart racing, face flushing, hands and jaw clench)*

- acknowledge that we have a choice between reacting *(which doesn't involve thought)* and responding *(which is calm and reasoned)*

- breathe deeply in and out a few times

- ask questions, drop assumptions, stay curious about the situation and why it upsets me

- ask myself what I'm afraid of and acknowledge that most fears don't ever come to pass

- identify my goal and ask my child what his/her goal is in this situation; can we find common ground?

- Express my feelings and own them *(I'm really angry right now v. You're pissing me off)*

ACTIVITY: Three Questions

When I am overwhelmed with emotion and tempted to lash out at my teen for something she did, I have learned to stop and ask myself these three questions before I start screaming or handing out punishments. (Credit: Brene Brown, "Daring Greatly")

1. *Do I have enough information about this situation to make a decision?*

   Almost every time, the answer is no. Especially if I have walked into a giant fight between my daughters or if I've only heard the teacher's side of the story, chances are I need more information. My child isn't always the most reliable source of information (she is, after all, biased toward her own story), but the best thing I can do to buy time before things blow up is to ask lots of questions.

2. *Am I fully present?*

   If the situation has taken me by surprise, the answer to this question is also generally, no. If I'm in the middle of making dinner or paying bills or rushing out the door and my daughters erupt into a screaming match, my brain is probably somewhere else and I will be more prone to irritation and impatience because I want to be doing something else. If I can't be fully present, stop what I'm doing, and pay 100% attention with a clear head and a calm demeanor right now, the best thing for me to do is to put off the conflict resolution or take a minute to get present. Nobody benefits from me being distracted and not paying attention.

3. *What am I afraid of?*

   This is a biggie, because it generally dictates what I say to my kids. It has taken practice, but the more I ask myself this question and really dig deep to find the answer, the more I understand how my fears drive my parenting. Some of the most common answers that come out of my head are:

   - Raising snotty, entitled kids

   - That someone is going to get physically injured

   - That this means I'm not a good mother/this is somehow my fault

   - That my kid will go somewhere and end up drunk/stoned/dead

More often than not, the things we fear are the things least likely to happen. Human beings tend to predict outcomes in best-case scenarios and in worst-case scenarios, when really, the things that happen most often happen somewhere in the middle. When I take a moment to assess my fears, I often have to laugh because they are so unrealistic. We hear so many stories about catastrophes — teens driving drunk, teen pregnancy, binge drinking, etc. — that we focus on those stories in our heads. We are driven to protect our kids from all sorts of things and the more independent they get, the more out of control we feel. If we feel as though we aren't in control, the first thing we try to do is close ranks and keep everyone nearby.

<u>Taking it Personally</u>

I don't think I'll ever forget the first time my daughter said the words, "I HATE you!" to me. It was awful. She was three years old. And while I can look back on it now and understand that she was working out ways to have power over me and get what she wanted and that she wasn't the most articulate when it came to expressing her feelings, at the time it really hurt. It took me years to figure out how to not take her attacks personally. The older she got, the better she got at pushing my buttons and saying things that she knew would hit at the core of who I am. If I follow my own teaching, though, I have to remember that the things people say and do are about *them*, not *me*. I have to remind myself that just because someone is angry with me or doesn't like me, that doesn't mean I am a horrible person at my core. Just because everyone doesn't love me all the time does not mean that I am unlovable. It is also important to remember that our children are emotional beings and what they feel right this very minute is likely to change soon. It is our job as parents to acknowledge their right to feel what they feel, maintain boundaries around how they treat us, and let them know that we love them no matter what.

I draw the line at hateful words and physical acts of violence, to be certain. I have been known to wait until my child is done yelling at me, calmly let them know that I do not deserve to be treated like that, and offer to listen to them later when they have let the strongest emotions pass and they are willing to have a respectful discussion. I have one daughter who is determined to "have it out" at the very moment she is upset and it can sometimes be a struggle to walk away and get her to leave me alone, but I know that when I set firm boundaries for myself I am setting the example for her that she can do the same. Generally it doesn't take long for her to calm down enough to apologize and ask to talk about the situation. My other daughter hates conflict so she tends to explode in anger and be done quickly. Often, when I check in with her later to see whether she wants to talk, she says she is "over it" and has already moved on.

When we take our children's words personally, we make the conflict much bigger because we become more invested in "winning" the argument than we do in solving the problem. Once both sides have identified with a particular idea to the point where they have internalized it, then the argument becomes about You v. Me and the real issue has been set aside and it is nearly impossible to find common ground. If one person (ideally, the adult in the situation) refuses to take it personally, it is harder to make the conflict about Right v. Wrong, and easier to have a rational discussion instead of pitting our hurt feelings against each other. It's hard and it takes lots of practice and there are times when I completely forget all of this sage advice, but I have learned that if I pay attention, it's possible to notice when I'm taking something personally. Generally, if I am

- Defensive
- Blaming
- Self-righteous

I am taking it personally. If I feel the need to justify why I have done something or if I am amazed at how much I am taken for granted or if I start a sentence with name-calling or put-downs, it's time to step back and remember **this is not about me**.

8 HELPING YOUR CHILD DEAL WITH STRESS AND ANXIETY

By many accounts, today's teens are more stressed out than any other generation in modern history. They are more plagued with depression and anxiety disorders, their rates of suicide and self-harm behaviors are unprecedented, and it's not really hard to understand why. Never before have there been so many standardized tests, the competition to get into college is heated and intense, rates of poverty have skyrocketed, and in many schools, the amount of homework amounts to multiple hours every night. Add to this the perfect storm of adolescent emotions, and you've got a recipe for stressed out kids. So how can we help them? What can we do to guide our kids through these challenging times with some semblance of calm?

<u>Understand and Explain the Brain's Dead-Ends and Antidotes</u>

There are certain thoughts and patterns that lead us to dead-ends, and the more we indulge those thoughts, the harder it gets to change them. If we wear pathways in our brains that lead us toward sadness and isolation, those are the pathways we will travel more and more. **What you practice grows stronger.** These dead ends come in the form of:

- Self-doubt
- Fear
- Scarcity (I'm not good enough, there isn't enough time…)
- Impatience
- Purposelessness (not taking the time to know where we're going or why)

I call them dead-ends because **when we find ourselves thinking these thoughts, we end up pushing ourselves away from other people**, dwelling on the negative possibilities, and reacting to others instead of responding to them. When we are not engaged with the people around us, we don't get other perspectives and we have a hard time seeing that there are other ideas and possibilities out there that might counteract our unhappy thoughts.

The good news is, there are antidotes to these thought patterns, and they can be easily accessed within ourselves. The more we practice substituting these thoughts for the dead end ones, the easier it gets. Every time you notice yourself or your child heading for a dead end, try one or more of these remedies:

- **Mindfulness without judgment** *I'm doubting myself or feeling afraid or impatient*
- **Self-compassion** *I'm human, so I'm bound to make mistakes. It's okay*
- **Purpose** *What are my goals? What are my values? How can I focus on those right now?*
- **Play** *Take a break to do something for the pure joy of it. Play unleashes creativity and helps us pay attention to something that won't be graded*
- **Mastery** *Remember that completing patterns or figuring something out gives us a hit of dopamine. Find something you know you're good at and do it for a little while. It will remind you that you are capable and strong.*

The things that offer us possibilities, open up ideas, and connect us to other people have a way of getting us out of those dead ends. The more we see the world open up to us with options, the happier we will be, and the next time we find ourselves in a place of doubt and uncertainty, we might just remember to open the toolbox that contains the antidotes.

Learn to Notice How Your Stress and Your Child's Stress Feed Each Other

I have two daughters whom I love deeply. While they are very different from each other and very different from me, I often find myself falling into the trap of feeling what they are feeling. One night, after a particularly challenging day filled with racing from work to school to after school activities, home to make dinner and clean up and feeling exhausted at the mere thought of facing another day of single-parenting, I was wiped out and looking forward to collapsing on the couch with the TV for some "me-time."

My youngest, then about 11 years old, called to me to sit with her for a few minutes while she fell asleep. She said she was having a hard time calming down enough to fall asleep. She was teary and whiny and I got snarky. I refused her request and headed off to tell her sister goodnight. My oldest, who had been sick with a pretty nasty cold for a couple of weeks, stuck her tongue out for me to examine as soon as I walked into her room. She wanted to know whether I thought there was something really wrong with her – she had a white rash covering most of her tongue. I sighed a deep, loud sigh, and told her it was nothing to worry about. I rolled my eyes as she detailed what she had learned about such things by Googling it online and worried that she was going to die of some mysterious disease if I didn't take her to the doctor tonight. She was clearly panicked, my youngest was still crying in her room, and I threw my hands up and walked out the door. We all went to bed unhappy that night.

In both cases, the real issue was my inability to identify my own stress and deal with it before I interacted with my children. My own stress weighed so heavily on my mind that I was unable to separate theirs out and basically piled it on top of my own and decided to deny it all in one fell swoop. Instead of sitting with my girls for a few minutes each, brainstorming ways to feel more in control and relaxed, I shut them out and walked away because I was uncomfortable.

ACTIVITY: Assess Your Stress

1. Can you recall times when you were unable to sympathize with your child because of your own stress level?

2. What are the things that trigger your stress reactions? What are your kids' triggers?

3. What do you think your baseline stress level is on an average day? What would your children or partner say it is?

4. How do you generally respond to feeling stressed? How do your kids and partner respond to your stress?

5. How can you try to set aside what is going on in your life when your children are in need of your help to de-stress? Is there something you can do or say to yourself that will allow you to help them without the weight of your own pressures for a little while?

Dealing With an Unexpected Event

We are taught that resisting change is one way to avoid stress. If we can just keep things predictable and avoid situations where we might not be in control, we think we are safe and secure. But there really is no such situation in life, which means that it is up to us to learn how to adapt to change and handle unexpected events that challenge us. It is an incredibly important skill for our children to learn as well. Dr. Dan Siegel has developed a set of steps that we can teach our kids when things don't go as planned and we start to get worried. These steps can be used for everything from getting disciplined by a coach for a mistake to getting a bad grade on a school project. It is pretty common for teens to not want to share their innermost thoughts and fears with others, but you can at least encourage them to go through the motions and, if they want to, write down their thoughts to save for the next time they're feeling blind-sided.

1. Ask yourself why you're upset about this.

2. Try not to react to your thoughts or emotions – just notice them as they float through your head

3. Understand that fear and anxiety are temporary. They won't be here forever and they don't define you as a person

4. Remember that if you don't fight them, emotions only last in your body for about 90 seconds. Let them pass over you like a wave

It is really tempting for us to commiserate with our kids when they're feeling upset, and often we do that by validating their "poor me" attitudes because we think it will feel supportive. We love to go to bat for our kids in many cases, and sometimes that's appropriate, but if you react to their disappointments with something like, "You're right, this isn't fair!" or "Anna was a horrible partner for that project – you did all the work," you're sending the message that they have no control over what happens to them in their lives, that life simply happens to us sometimes and there's nothing we can do about it. That is setting them up for a pretty awful view of what might come. If you offer to rush in and fix things for them, you're sending the message that they can't do it on their own and that they shouldn't have to. If you help them acknowledge their feelings without using them as an excuse to give up or get angry, you can help guide them to a place where they can discover the lesson in what happened and move on.

ACTIVITY: Meditation – Leaves in a Stream

Go to www.theSELFProject.com and click on the link for the guided meditation. It is a short, five minute exercise that can help you or your child practice letting go of strong emotions and the thoughts we link to them. The more you practice, the easier it gets to move past anger and frustration and come to a place of calm.

ACTIVITY: Tackling Tough Situations

Sometimes when we find ourselves in a place that is challenging, we react in anger or frustration. Other times, we are tempted to shove our unhappy feelings aside and keep going, but that rarely works for long. The next time your child is struggling with a difficult situation, sit down with them and take a look at this worksheet. The first two boxes are designed to simply outline what is going on and to bring some awareness of the emotional reactions your child is having. As your child makes their way through the flow chart, they begin to see that they can make choices about how to respond to the situation. It is a powerful, but quick, reminder that we are always in charge of how we deal with things that come up in our lives. In the end, they make a conscious decision either to accept what has happened and move on or reach out for assistance so that they can change things for the better.

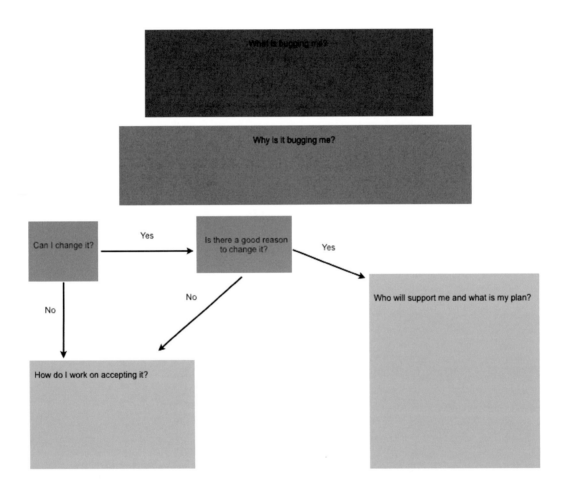

Help Your Child Find the Meaning in their Life

Adolescents are inundated with goals on a daily basis. Unfortunately, most of those goals come from external sources – coaches, teachers, parents, employers. If they are to be "successful" they have to live up to many different standards set by other people and it can often be hard to identify what is really important to them. When you're surrounded by people who are telling you what you "ought" to be doing, it is easy to go on autopilot and become out of touch with your own motivations and values. Ironically, though, there is a lot of research that shows that we feel better about what we're doing when it is tied to an internal purpose. Some people have called this The IKEA Effect - that we value things much more if we made them ourselves or had some hand in their creation. As a parent, you can help your child gain a sense of ownership and power over their daily choices by helping them define their values and goals. Framing conversations in terms of values is a great way to bring your kids back to why what they're doing matters and helps them decide where they truly want to focus their time and energy.

ACTIVITY: Do Your Activities Have Meaning?

Sit down with your child and discuss your answers to these questions. This is a great way for both of you to think about how you spend your time and why.

- How much of your day is spent doing things you don't feel are important? How often do you do things to please others without being really invested in the outcome?

- Do you think you are more internally or externally motivated? Does it depend on what you're doing? If there are times where it varies, can you see a difference in your level of enthusiasm for a task when you're doing something creative or 'meaningful?'

- When you are stressed or anxious, is it generally due to an expectation someone else has for you?

ACTIVITY: Help Your Child Plan for Success

Sometimes, even when we know what is important to us, it is hard to know exactly how to go about expressing that in our lives. I am a big fan of goal-setting, especially when I can feel myself getting worried about an upcoming deadline that means a lot to me. The following activity is easy to adapt to a wide range of short-term goals and I have included some examples of potential answers for you to see. The next time your child is feeling stressed about something they have to do, have them try this exercise.

1. Set an achievable goal.

   I want to get an A on my next term paper. I want to get more assists in the next basketball game.

2. What will happen if I achieve this goal?

   My parents will stop nagging me and see that I'm working hard. I might make varsity next year.

3. Why is this goal important to me?

   I want my parents to trust that I'm serious about my education. I really love basketball and the varsity coach can help me develop my skills.

4. Be realistic about what it will take. Identify potential obstacles and plan for them. Build in flexibility.
   I have to work after school this week and we are going away this weekend, so I'll have to find time to really prepare for the paper. I might not play a lot in the next game, but maybe if I tell the coach my goal, he'll put me in more.

5. Decide what realistic progress looks like.

   I got a C on my last paper, so even if I get a B this time, I will know that I've improved and keep working. Even if I get the same number of assists or just one more next time, I'll know I'm on the right track.

This is a great way to help your child understand that they have the power to make important changes in their own life. When we are very clear on what we want and why we want it, we can go forward with conviction. Being honest about our abilities and the obstacles in our way helps us plan for flexibility and feel like we are in charge. When we are empowered to make choices based on what is important to us, we are happier and more likely to deal with setbacks positively.

<u>Help Your Child Understand That They are Part of Something Bigger</u>

Adolescents often get lost in their own world, thinking mostly of themselves and worrying about how everyone else might see them. Developmentally, this is a normal phenomenon, but the longer you live inside your own mind, the easier it is to believe everything you think, and when you're stressed and anxious, that isn't helpful. Getting out and being social with supportive, nonjudgmental friends and family goes a long way toward alleviating some of that stress, but for many kids, offering kindness to others is a powerful tool as well. Altriustic acts can be as simple as holding the door for another student who is on crutches or tossing your extra change on the counter when the person in front of you at the coffee shop is a few cents short, and they can be more elaborate, including community service projects. Evidence shows that the kinder we are to others, the more forgiving we are of ourselves, and the happier we are. Often, all it takes is a few small kindnesses to remind us how good it feels to help others, and the following activity is one you can do at home to kickstart the process for your kids.

ACTIVITY: Weekly Gifts

Put a slip of paper with the name of each person in your household in a hat or bowl. Designate one time a week – Sunday dinner, for example – when each person reaches in and takes the name of a different person. I try to keep it anonymous, but you can share the information if you choose. Everyone has one week to do something nice for the person whose name they drew. Examples can be things like:

- Clearing their dishes from the dinner table

- Folding a load of laundry for them

- Making a cup of tea just the way they like it

- Offering to take on a chore like walking the dog when it isn't your turn because you can see that the other person is really busy

- Letting them have the shower first without arguing

Encourage everyone to be creative. Along with the obvious benefit of knowing that someone will do something nice for you at least once this week, this exercise focuses attention outside ourselves and prompts us to pay attention to what is going on in other people's lives, what is important to them. You will find yourself asking, 'What could I do to help _____ the most today?' This exercise builds empathy and understanding and it creates stronger connections between family members.

Encourage Gratitude

Because of the way our brains are wired, we often focus more on the negative things in our lives than we do on the positive. Fortunately, like everything else I've talked about here, gratitude gets easier the more we practice it, even if we are thinking about what we're grateful for when things are going pretty well.

I started my own gratitude practice several years ago in an effort to ward off depression. When I was really wrestling with stress, anxiety and fear, mornings were the worst time for me. I often woke up opening one eye at a time as I tried to determine whether a trainload of pain and longing was headed for me before my feet hid the floor. A friend suggested that even before I open my eyes, I start by making a list of things for which I am truly grateful as a sort of shield against the negative thoughts. I figured it couldn't hurt.

In the beginning it was hard for me to come up with a list. Not because I don't have many, many blessings in my life, but because I have a tendency to qualify them. As soon as I think of one, I either compare it to someone else and feel guilty that I have more than someone else, or I determine that it sounds ridiculous and petty, like being grateful that I have enough money to pay my bills. It took me a little while to figure out that gratitude has nothing to do with comparisons. It never starts with, "at least I'm not…" If I'm comparing my life to someone else's or thinking about all the ways things could be worse, I'm not going to feel better.

Gratitude also isn't a balance sheet. I don't advocate weighing the "good" things in my life against the number or magnitude of "bad" things. Gratitude stands on its own. This may make it sound hard, but once you get going it really isn't. When I get frustrated or irritable, the best thing for me to do is take a deep breath and look around. I see my computer and I'm grateful for the ability to use it to connect to important ideas and people online. I catch sight of a glass of water and thank goodness for clean water to drink and bathe in. I see my sunglasses lying on the counter and smile at the thought of warm sunshine on my back. There is no attempt to think beyond these simple things and if I take a minute or five to just focus on them without going beyond those thoughts, I generally feel much better.

ACTIVITY: Daily Gratitude Practice

When my oldest daughter started high school, she found herself feeling really anxious a few times a week. She went to a school where she didn't know anyone and the culture was very different from the school she had attended before. She felt scared, out of place, and lonely. It didn't take long before she began asking me to let her stay home and skip first period or pick her up early. One of the best things we did to combat this was to start a gratitude practice. Every night before she fell asleep, I asked her to text me three things for which she was grateful. If she was having a hard time thinking of anything, I sent her my three first. They were pretty basic, and often included things like flannel sheets, soft pillows, the dog snoring at the foot of the bed, or remembering a joke the two of us shared earlier that day. Within a week, she was texting me her three without any prompting, and within two weeks, the things she listed were more insightful and deeper.

The reasons I had her text me were twofold; first, I knew that she would be more comfortable sharing if we weren't looking at each other; second, it didn't encourage a conversation or any sort of judgment about her choices or mine. There were no facial expressions to interpret so she didn't have to worry about my reaction. But perhaps the best part of this was that, as she lay in bed texting me right before she turned out her light and went to sleep, the last thing she saw and thought about were three things that make her happy, and that was a pretty powerful way to shift the way she was thinking when the only task ahead of her was to get some rest.

None of these activities or ideas is meant to be a substitute for counseling or intervention by trained medical professionals. If your child is struggling with fear and anxiety to the point where they are unable to find meaning and purpose and function on a daily basis, please seek additional help.

The SELF Project curriculum for kids contains several more activities and meditations that you may be interested in seeing as you strive to help your child navigate these difficult years. Our website also has guided meditations that are available to use any time.

You can visit us at www.theSELFProject.com or like our Facebook page.

ABOUT THE AUTHOR

Kari O'Driscoll is the mother of two teenage daughters and a former healthcare professional. She has written extensively about parenting, social justice and mindfulness for online and print publications. She is convinced that the more work we do in community to support each others' emotional health, the better off we will all be.

67356767R00027

Made in the USA
Lexington, KY
09 September 2017